D1593961

This copy of

SING TO THE LORD

comes to

_____

with love from

_____

SING TO THE LORD

Copyright © 1996 by Eagle

Published by Crossway Books
a division of Good News Publishers
1300 Crescent Street
Wheaton, Illinois 60187

First British edition published by Eagle, 1996

First U.S. edition published by Crossway Books, 1998

First U.S. printing, 1998

Printed in Singapore

Song Copyrights
"All Heaven Declares," © Thankyou Music, 1987.
"You Laid Aside Your Majesty," © Thankyou Music, 1985.
"River Wash Over Me," © Thankyou Music, 1980.
"How Great Thou Art!" © Stuart K. Hine/Thankyou Music, 1953.
"Shine, Jesus, Shine," © Make Way Music, 1987.

LIBRARY OF CONGRESS CATALOGING-IN-PUBLICATION DATA
Sing to the Lord : well-loved hymns and choruses. — 1st U.S. ed.
    p.   cm.
  1. Hymns, English—Texts.   I. Crossway Books.
BV350.S55 1998   264'.23—dc21   97-38454
ISBN 0-89107-989-0

08	07	06	05	04	03	02	01	00	99	98
15	14	13	12	11	10	9	8	7	6	5	4	3	2	1

Sing to the Lord

Well-Loved Hymns and Choruses

❧

CROSSWAY BOOKS

ALL HEAVEN DECLARES

NOEL AND TRICIA RICHARDS

All heaven declares
The glory of the risen Lord.
Who can compare
With the beauty of the Lord?
Forever He will be
The Lamb upon the throne.
I gladly bow the knee
And worship Him alone.

I will proclaim
The glory of the risen Lord,
Who once was slain
To reconcile man to God.
Forever You will be
The Lamb upon the throne.
I gladly bow the knee
And worship You alone.

A Glorious Sunset, John Brett

AMAZING GRACE

JOHN NEWTON

Amazing grace! how sweet the sound
That saved a wretch like me;
I once was lost, but now am found,
Was blind, but now I see.

'Twas grace that taught my heart to fear,
And grace my fears relieved;
How precious did that grace appear,
The hour I first believed!

Through many dangers, toils, and snares
I have already come;
'Tis grace that brought me safe thus far,
And grace will lead me home.

When we've been there ten thousand years,
Bright shining as the sun,
We've no less days to sing God's praise
Than when we first begun.

The Artist's Wife in Their Garden, Paul-Leon Frequenez

YOU LAID ASIDE YOUR MAJESTY

NOEL RICHARDS

You laid aside Your majesty,
Gave up everything for me,
Suffered at the hands of those You had created.
You took all my guilt and shame,
When You died and rose again;
Now today You reign,
In heaven and earth exalted.

I really want to worship You, my Lord,
You have won my heart
And I am Yours for ever and ever;
I will love You.
You are the only one who died for me,
Gave Your life to set me free,
So I lift my voice to You in adoration.

Un jour en été, Henri-Gatson Darien

IMMORTAL, INVISIBLE, GOD ONLY WISE

WALTER CHALMERS SMITH

Immortal, invisible, God only wise,
In light inaccessible hid from our eyes,
Most blessed, most glorious, the Ancient of Days,
Almighty, victorious, Thy great name we praise.

Unresting, unhasting, and silent as light,
Nor wanting nor wasting, Thou rulest in might;
Thy justice like mountains, high soaring above
Thy clouds which are fountains of goodness and love.

To all life Thou givest, to both great and small;
In all life Thou livest, the true life of all;
We blossom and flourish as leaves on the tree,
And wither and perish; but naught changeth Thee.

Great Father of glory, pure Father of light,
Thine angels adore Thee, all veiling their sight;
All laud we would render: O help us to see
'Tis only the splendor of light hideth Thee.

Billing and Cooing, Carl Vilhelm Balsgaard

RIVER WASH OVER ME

DOUGIE BROWN

River wash over me,
Cleanse me and make me new.
Bathe me, refresh me and fill me anew,
River wash over me.

Spirit watch over me,
Lead me to Jesus' feet.
Cause me to worship and fill me anew,
Spirit wash over me.

Jesus rule over me,
Reign over all my heart.
Teach me to praise You and fill me anew,
Jesus rule over me.

A Bend in the River, Benjamin Williams Leader

HOW GREAT THOU ART!

STUART K. HINE

O Lord my God! when I in awesome wonder
Consider all the works Thy hand hath made,
I see the stars, I hear the mighty thunder,
Thy power throughout the universe displayed:

> Then sings my soul, my Savior God, to Thee,
> How great Thou art! How great Thou art!
> Then sings my soul, my Savior God, to Thee,
> How great Thou art! How great Thou art!

When through the woods and forest glades I wander
And hear the birds sing sweetly in the trees;
When I look down from lofty mountain grandeur,
And hear the brook, and feel the gentle breeze;

And when I think that God His Son not sparing,
Sent Him to die—I scarce can take it in.
That on the cross my burden gladly bearing,
He bled and died to take away my sin:

When Christ shall come with shout of acclamation
And take me home—what joy shall fill my heart!
Then I shall bow in humble adoration
And there proclaim, my God, how great Thou art!

Where Tranquility Lies, Alfred Oliver

O JESUS, I HAVE PROMISED

JOHN EARNEST BODE

O Jesus, I have promised
To serve Thee to the end;
Be Thou forever near me,
My Master and my Friend;
I shall not fear the battle
If Thou art by my side,
Nor wander from the pathway
If Thou wilt be my Guide.

O let me hear Thee speaking
In accents clear and still,
Above the storms of passion,
The murmurs of self-will;
O speak to reassure me,
To hasten, or control;
O speak, and make me listen,
Thou Guardian of my soul.

O Jesus, thou hast promised
To all who follow Thee
That where Thou art in glory
There shall Thy servants be;
And, Jesus, I have promised
To serve Thee to the end;
O give me grace to follow,
My Master and my Friend.

A View of Runnymede and Windsor, Edmund John Niemann

JUST AS I AM

CHARLOTTE ELLIOT

Just as I am, without one plea
But that Thy blood was shed for me,
And that Thou bid'st me come to Thee,
O Lamb of God, I come.

Just as I am, and waiting not
To rid my soul of one dark blot,
To Thee, whose blood can cleanse each spot,
O Lamb of God, I come.

Just as I am, though tossed about
With many a conflict, many a doubt,
Fightings and fears within, without,
O Lamb of God, I come.

Just as I am, Thou wilt receive,
Wilt welcome, pardon, cleanse, relieve;
Because Thy promise I believe,
O Lamb of God, I come.

Just as I am, of that free love
The breadth, length, depth and height to prove,
Here for a season, then above,
O Lamb of God, I come.

Picking Honeysuckle, Sophie Anderson

HERE IS LOVE VAST AS THE OCEAN

ROBERT LOWRY

Here is love vast as the ocean,
Loving kindness as the flood,
When the Prince of Life, our ransom
Shed for us His precious blood.
Who His love will not remember?
Who can cease to sing His praise?
He can never be forgotten
Throughout heaven's eternal days.

On the Mount of Crucifixion
Fountains opened deep and wide;
Through the floodgates of God's mercy
Flowed a vast and gracious tide.
Grace and love, like mighty rivers,
Poured incessant from above,
And heaven's peace and perfect justice
Kissed a guilty world in love.

Sandy Shore, 1891, Benjamin Williams Leader

SHINE, JESUS, SHINE

GRAHAM KENDRICK

Lord, the light of Your love is shining,
In the midst of the darkness, shining;
Jesus, Light of the world, shine upon us,
Set us free by the truth You now bring us.
Shine on me, shine on me.

Shine, Jesus, shine,
Fill this land with the Father's glory;
Blaze, Spirit, blaze,
Set our hearts on fire.
Flow, river, flow,
Flood the nations with grace and mercy;
Send forth Your word, Lord, and let there be light.

Lord, I come to Your awesome presence,
From the shadows into Your radiance;
By the blood I may enter Your brightness,
Search me, try me, consume all my darkness.
Shine on me, shine on me.

As we gaze on Your kingly brightness
So our faces display Your likeness.
Ever changing from glory to glory,
Mirrored here may our lives tell Your story.
Shine on me, shine on me.

Greenwich Hospital, 1878, James Francis Danby

O GOD, OUR HELP IN AGES PAST

ISAAC WATTS

O God, our help in ages past,
Our hope for years to come,
Our shelter from the stormy blast,
And our eternal home.

Under the shadow of Thy throne
Thy saints have dwelt secure;
Sufficient is Thine arm alone,
And our defense is sure.

Before the hills in order stood,
Or earth received her frame,
From everlasting Thou art God,
To endless years the same.

A thousand ages, in Thy sight,
Are like an evening gone;
Short as the watch that ends the night,
Before the rising sun.

Time, like an ever-rolling stream,
Bears all its sons away;
They fly forgotten, as a dream
Dies at the opening day.

O God, our help in ages past,
Our hope for years to come,
Be Thou our guard while life shall last,
And our eternal home.

The Marsh at Sunset, Lucien Frank

THE DAY THOU GAVEST, LORD, IS ENDED

JOHN ELLERTON

The day Thou gavest, Lord, is ended,
The darkness falls at Thy behest;
To Thee our morning hymns ascended,
Thy praise shall sanctify our rest.

We thank Thee that Thy church unsleeping,
While earth rolls onward into light,
Through all the world her watch is keeping,
And rests not now by day or night.

As o'er each continent and island
The dawn leads on another day,
The voice of prayer is never silent,
Nor dies the strain of praise away.

The sun that bids us rest is waking
Our brethren 'neath the western sky,
And hour by hour fresh lips are making
Thy wondrous doings heard on high.

So be it, Lord! Thy throne shall never,
Like earth's proud empires, pass away;
Thy kingdom stands, and grows forever,
Till all Thy creatures own Thy sway.

Hazy Sunshine (sunset), Albert Gabriel Rigolot

AND CAN IT BE?

CHARLES WESLEY

And can it be that I should gain
An interest in the Savior's blood?
Died He for me, who caused His pain?
For me, who Him to death pursued?
Amazing love! how can it be
That Thou, my God, shouldst die for me?

He left His Father's throne above,
So free, so infinite His grace;
Emptied Himself of all but love,
And bled for Adam's helpless race.
'Tis mercy all, immense and free;
For, O my God, it found out me.

Long my imprisoned spirit lay
Fast bound in sin and nature's night;
Thine eyes diffused a quickening ray,
I woke, the dungeon flamed with light;
My chains fell off, my heart was free;
I rose, went forth, and followed Thee.

No condemnation now I dread;
Jesus, and all in Him, is mine!
Alive in Him, my living Head,
And clothed in righteousness divine,
Bold I approach the eternal throne,
And claim the crown, through Christ my own.

Picking Flowers in an Alpine Meadow, Hans Dahl

1894

WHAT A FRIEND WE HAVE IN JESUS

JOSEPH M. SCRIVEN

What a friend we have in Jesus,
All our sins and griefs to bear!
What a privilege to carry
Everything to God in prayer!
O what peace we often forfeit!
O what needless pain we bear!
All because we do not carry
Everything to God in prayer.

Have we trials and temptations?
Is there trouble anywhere?
We should never be discouraged;
Take it to the Lord in prayer.
Can we find a friend so faithful
Who will all our sorrows share?
Jesus knows our every weakness;
Take it to the Lord in prayer.

Are we weak and heavy-laden,
Cumbered with a load of care?
Precious Savior, still our refuge,
Take it to the Lord in prayer.
Do thy friends despise, forsake thee?
Take it to the Lord in prayer;
In His arms He'll take and shield thee,
Thou wilt find a solace there.

An Afternoon by Lake Geneva, Frederic Dufaux

Photographic Credits

Crossway Books is grateful to the copyright holders listed below, and to The Bridgeman Art Library and The Fine Art Photographic Library in particular for their kind permission to reproduce the paintings selected to complement the text.

COVER *An Afternoon by Lake Geneva,* by Frederic Dufaux, 1852-1943, Galerie George.

1. *A Glorious Sunset,* by John Brett, 1830-1902, Private Collection.

2. *The Artist's Wife in Their Garden,* by Paul-Leon Frenquenez, 1876-1943, Waterhouse & Dodd, London.

3. *Un jour en été,* by Henri-Gatson Darien, 1864-1926, Galerie Berko.

4. *Billing and Cooing,* by Carl Vilhelm Balsgaard, 1812-1893, Apollo Gallery.

5. *A Bend in the River,* by Benjamin Williams Leader, 1831-1923.

6. *Where Tranquility Lies,* by Alfred Oliver, ?-1943, Private Collection.

7. *A View of Runnymede and Windsor,* by Edmund John Niemann, 1813-1876, Colin Stodgell Gallery.

8. *Picking Honeysuckle,* by Sophie Anderson, 1823-1898.

9. *Sandy Shore, 1891,* by Benjamin Williams Leader, 1831-1923.

10. *Greenwich Hospital, 1878,* by James Francis Danby, 1816-1875.

11. *The Marsh at Sunset,* by Lucien Frank, 1857-1920, Galerie Berko.

12. *Hazy Sunshine (sunset),* by Albert Gabriel Rigolot, 1862-1932, Eaton Gallery, London.

13. *Picking Flowers in an Alpine Meadow,* by Hans Dahl, 1849-1937, Polak Gallery, London.

14. *An Afternoon by Lake Geneva,* by Frederic Dufaux, 1852-1943, Galerie George.